ATLANTA BRAVES

by Brian Howell

Published by ABDO Publishing Company, 8000 West 78th Street, Edina, Minnesota 55439. Copyright © 2011 by Abdo Consulting Group, Inc. International copyrights reserved in all countries. No part of this book may be reproduced in any form without written permission from the publisher. SportsZone™ is a trademark and logo of ABDO Publishing Company.

Printed in the United States of America,
North Mankato, Minnesota
112010
012011

 THIS BOOK CONTAINS AT LEAST 10% RECYCLED MATERIALS.

Editor: Chrös McDougall
Copy Editor: Nicholas Cafarelli
Interior Design and Production: Carol Castro
Cover Design: Christa Schneider

Photo Credits: John Bazemore/AP Images, cover; AP Images, 1, 4, 7, 9, 15, 16, 18, 21, 25, 31, 42 (middle and bottom), 43 (top); George H. Hastings, 10, 42 (top); Bain News Service/Library of Congress, 12; Harry L. Hall/AP Images, 22; RHH/AP Images, 26; File/AP Images, 28; Rusty Kennedy/AP Images, 32; Jim Mone/AP Images, 35; Doug Mills/AP Images, 37; Ed Reinke/AP Images, 38, 43 (middle); Curtis Compton/Atlanta Journal-Constitution/AP Images, 41, 43 (bottom); Jeff Roberson/AP Images, 44; Ric Feld/AP Images, 47

Library of Congress Cataloging-in-Publication Data
Howell, Brian, 1974-
 Atlanta Braves / by Brian Howell.
  p. cm. — (Inside MLB)
 ISBN 978-1-61714-035-8
 1. Atlanta Braves (Baseball team)—History—Juvenile Literature. I. Title.
 GV875.A8H69 2011
 796.357'6409758231—dc22
                    2010036555

TABLE OF CONTENTS

CHAPTER 1

HAMMERIN' HANK

Growing up in Alabama, Henry "Hank" Aaron always found a way to play baseball—even when he did not have a bat and ball. He would hit bottle caps with a broomstick if he had to, and he and his brothers found creative ways to make baseballs.

"We'd make our own baseballs by wrapping nylon hose around an old golf ball, or just use old rags tied together, or handlebar grips, or tin cans crumpled up," he said.

Hank had chores to do, also, but his focus was often on baseball. "When I look back on my life, I can see that all through my childhood I was being prepared to play baseball," he said.

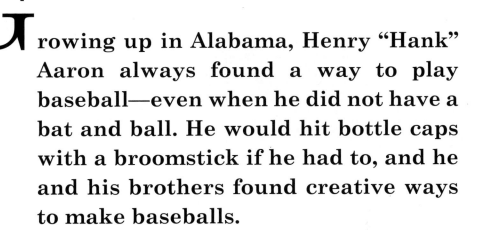

High Praise

Joe Adcock, who played for the Braves from 1953 to 1962, was also a very good hitter. He was quite impressed with Hank Aaron, however. "Trying to sneak a pitch past Hank Aaron is like trying to sneak the sunrise past a rooster," he said.

Hank Aaron played for the Milwaukee and Atlanta Braves from 1954 to 1974. He was an All-Star in all but his first season with the Braves.

EARLY START

Henry "Hank" Aaron signed with the Indianapolis Clowns of the Negro Leagues in 1952. He was 18 years old that season. He signed with the Braves later in 1952 and, after a couple of seasons in the minor leagues, he became a major league player in 1954.

Aaron is well known for the home-run record he owned for 33 years. The Alabama native was much more than a power hitter, however. Aaron was an All-Star in 21 straight seasons (1955–75) and won the National League (NL) Most Valuable Player (MVP) Award in 1957. He finished with a career .305 batting average and 3,771 hits. He also won two batting titles. He holds major league records for runs batted in (2,297) and total bases (6,856). During his career, Aaron also showed his speed (240 career stolen bases) and was a stellar outfielder, winning three Gold Gloves.

On the night of April 8, 1974, Aaron was far away from his Alabama childhood. No longer the little boy hitting bottle caps, Aaron was a star for the Atlanta Braves. That night, he walked to the plate in Atlanta-Fulton County Stadium as a 40-year-old man with 714 career home runs. That tied him with legendary Babe Ruth for the most home runs in baseball history.

During the fourth inning, Al Downing of the Los Angeles Dodgers threw a fastball to Aaron. "Hammerin' Hank," as he was known, swung hard, and hit the ball over the fence for a home run. It was the 715th homer of his career, making him baseball's all-time home-run king.

"I was in my own little world at the time," Aaron said of rounding the bases. "It was like I was running in a bubble

Hank Aaron hits his 715th home run to break Babe Ruth's career home-run record on April 8, 1974.

and I could see all these people jumping up and down and waving their arms in slow motion. . . . I was told I had a big smile on my face as I came around third. I purposely never smiled as I ran the bases after a home run, but I suppose I couldn't help it that time."

For Aaron, who is an African American, that home

Surprising Power

Through the 2010 season, players had slugged 50 or more home runs in a season only 42 times. Babe Ruth had four 50-homer seasons when he was playing in the 1920s. Hank Aaron, on the other hand, never had a 50-home-run season. His career high was 47 in 1971. Aaron was consistent, however: he had eight 40-home-run seasons and seven more with at least 30 homers.

run was the end of a long and difficult journey. Many people did not want to see him break the record. Ruth was a beloved figure in baseball history. Aaron was 18 years old when he became a professional baseball player in 1952. That was just five years after Jackie Robinson became the first black player in the major leagues. Even in 1974, not all fans had fully accepted black players.

In chasing Ruth's record, Aaron had to handle a great deal of pressure—both positive and negative—from the media and fans. When the chase was over, Aaron felt relieved. "I just thank God it's all over," he said. "I feel I can relax now. I feel my teammates can relax. I feel I can have a great season."

Aaron hit 20 home runs that season. When it was over, he was traded to the Milwaukee Brewers, for whom he played his final two seasons. He retired in 1976 with a record 755 home runs. That record stood until 2007, when Barry Bonds passed him. Although he is no longer officially the home-run king, Aaron is, in the eyes of many, one of the greatest players in baseball history. Without question, he was one of the greatest players in the history of the Atlanta Braves.

Teammates congratulate the newly-crowned home-run king, Hank Aaron, after he hit his 715th home run in 1974.

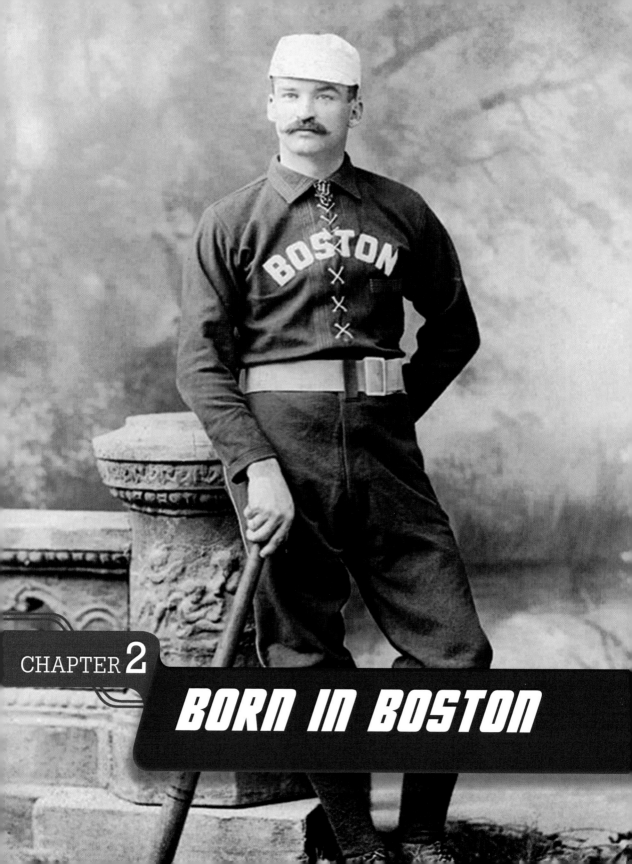

CHAPTER 2

BORN IN BOSTON

The Braves are the oldest active franchise in baseball. In fact, their first season was in 1876. The team is now settled in Atlanta, Georgia, but the Braves actually spent more time in Boston, Massachusetts.

One of the first professional baseball leagues was the National Association. The dominant team of that league was the Boston Red Stockings. They won the championship four straight years, from 1872 to 1875. Following that 1875 season, however, the National Association folded and the

Tough Boys

During the early days of professional baseball, teams could only substitute players in case of an injury. Because of that, the 1878 Boston Red Caps, who were the NL champions, used only 10 players all season. Harry Schafer was the only substitute the Red Caps used that season, and he played in just two of the team's 60 games.

Michael "King" Kelly played for the Boston Beaneaters in the 1880s and 1890s. He was inducted into the Baseball Hall of Fame in 1945.

From left, catcher Hank Gowdy, pitcher Lefty Tyler, and outfielder Joey Connolly relax during the Braves' 1914 pennant run.

National League was formed. The Red Stockings joined the NL to become the Boston Red Caps in 1876. That was the first official season of the team that would later be known as the Braves.

Beginning in 1876, the team that became the Braves played 77 seasons in Boston. It went by several nicknames during that time. They included the Red Caps, the Beaneaters, the Doves, the Pilgrims, and the Bees. They officially became the Braves in 1912. From 1936 to 1940, they were known as the Bees. But other than that, they have been called the Braves since 1912.

No matter what nickname they had, the team was one of the NL's best in the early years. From 1876 to 1900, the Braves organization won eight NL pennants, including three in a row from 1891 to 1893. Some of the best players of the nineteenth century suited up for those Boston teams. Hall of Famers John Clarkson, Jimmy Collins, Hugh Duffy, Billy Hamilton, Michael "King" Kelly, Tommy McCarthy, Charles "Kid" Nichols, and Vic Willis were among the first stars in team history.

When baseball entered the twentieth century, the Braves were hit with changes. The American League (AL) was formed in 1901. That gave the Braves some company in Boston, as the Red Sox were a part of the AL. The turn of the century also began a series of losing seasons for the Braves.

BASEBALL PIONEERS

Hall of Famer Harry Wright played a major role in baseball becoming a professional sport in the late 1800s. He was the manager of the Boston Red Stockings of the National Association, which folded after the 1875 season. He was then the first manager of the Braves organization, from 1876 to 1881. He led the team to two NL championships. He was inducted into the Baseball Hall of Fame in 1953.

Wright's brother, George, was also a baseball pioneer and a 1937 Hall of Fame inductee. George played infield for the Braves organization from 1876 to 1878 and from 1880 to 1881. George and Harry were the first set of brothers to be enshrined in the Hall of Fame. Their younger brother, Sam, played two games for the Red Caps in 1876.

In fact, they had 11 consecutive losing seasons from 1903 to 1913.

The Braves were in last place in the NL midway through the 1914 season. They appeared headed for another losing season. Then, they won 68 of their final 87 games to claim the NL pennant. Completing one of the greatest comebacks in baseball history, the Braves swept the heavily favored AL champion Philadelphia Athletics 4–0 to win the World Series. Catcher Hank Gowdy was one of the Braves' stars during the Series. He hit .545 in the four games.

The Braves finished off the four-game series with a 3–1 win at Fenway Park. They played the game at the neighboring Red Sox's stadium because it was larger than their home park. The fans went crazy.

"Cheering throngs piled out of the stands and bleachers and rushed across the field to the Boston bench," one newspaper wrote. "Gowdy, [Rabbit] Maranville, Captain [Johnny] Evers, and other heroes of the Series were lifted on the fans' shoulders while a roar of applause went up that could be heard on Boston commons."

The Braves finished second in the NL in 1915, one year after their World Series triumph.

Little Big Man

For nearly a decade in the early 1900s, one of the Braves' best players was one of their smallest. Walter James Vincent "Rabbit" Maranville stood just 5 feet, 5 inches tall and weighed only 155 pounds. He was a good hitter, but was also known for his defense and leadership. Maranville played for the Braves from 1912 to 1920 and from 1929 to 1935. His 103 triples still rank as the most in team history. Among Hall of Famers who played during the twentieth century, Maranville was the smallest.

Braves shortstop Al Dark watches to see if his throw completed a double play against the Cleveland Indians in Game 2 of the 1948 World Series.

But they never finished higher than third from 1916 to 1947. The Braves showed signs of improvement in 1947, however, and had a star player in Bob Elliott. He was named the NL's MVP that season.

The next season, the Braves finally ended their post-season drought. Just as they did in 1914, the Braves got off to a

Triple the Fun

On October 6, 1923, Braves short-stop Ernie Padgett was playing in only the fourth major league game of his career. He made it a memorable one when he turned an unassisted triple play—a play in which one defender records three outs. There have been only 15 in baseball history, and two of those were accomplished by the Braves. Shortstop Rafael Furcal joined the short list on August 10, 2003.

slow start. Through 38 games, they sat in fifth place. But eight days later, they were in first place. The Braves stayed there for all but one day during the rest of the season. After taking the NL championship, the Braves played the AL-champion Cleveland Indians in the World Series. However, the Braves lost four games to two.

The 1948 Braves were led by pitchers Warren Spahn and Johnny Sain. That season, Sain led the NL with 24 wins. Spahn, meanwhile, won 15 games. The duo was so much better than the other Braves pitchers that fans came up with a slogan, "Spahn and Sain and two days of rain." That meant they hoped for enough rainouts that the two aces would be rested and be able to pitch every game.

Spahn and Sain were not the only good players on the 1948 Braves team, however. Shortstop Al Dark was voted the NL's Rookie of the Year. And third baseman Elliott followed up his MVP season with another great year.

The Braves would play just four more years in Boston after the 1948 World Series. By 1952, the Red Sox had taken over as Boston's most popular team. They drew four times as many fans to Fenway Park as the Braves attracted to Braves Field. Braves owner Lou Perini did not want to share the city. After the 1952 season, he moved his team west to Milwaukee, Wisconsin. After 77 years in Boston, the Braves were embarking on a new era.

Pitchers Warren Spahn, *left*, and Johnny Sain carried the Boston Braves to the 1948 World Series, but the Braves lost to the Cleveland Indians.

CHAPTER 3

MOVING WEST, THEN SOUTH

During the spring of 1953, Braves owner Lou Perini announced his plans to move the team from Boston to Milwaukee. The Braves had shared Boston with the Red Sox for more than 50 years. "I arrived at the conclusion because enthusiasm in Boston is on the wane. If the people of Boston are not interested in the Braves, then we must move. I think Boston no longer is a two-team city," Perini said.

For the first time since 1901, the city of Milwaukee would have a Major League Baseball (MLB) team. And for the team, a new $5 million stadium awaited. Fans were excited, and the night before the first game, 1,500 fans greeted the team at the airport.

On April 14, 1953, the Braves played their first game in Milwaukee. Rookie center fielder Bill Bruton was the hero. He hit a ball that bounced off

Third baseman Eddie Mathews, *left*, chats with Brooklyn Dodgers catcher Roy Campanella in 1953. Mathews starred for the Braves from 1952 to 1966, playing in Boston, Milwaukee, and Atlanta.

the glove of St. Louis Cardinals right fielder Enos Slaughter and over the fence for a game-winning home run. It was Bruton's only home run of the season, and the Braves won 3–2. "I didn't look to see what the ball was doing," Bruton said. "I just kept on running."

That was the beginning of 13 seasons in Milwaukee.

Welcoming the Braves

More than 36,000 fans showed up to Milwaukee County Stadium for the Braves' game on April 14, 1953. It was the first major league game in Milwaukee in 52 years. "The Milwaukee Braves opened their home big-league season here Tuesday afternoon with a game that the capacity crowd will remember for a long time," Wisconsin State Journal columnist Henry J. McCormick wrote the next day. "This was an historic opening day." In 1953, the Braves set a NL attendance record, drawing more than 1.8 million fans. More than 2 million fans turned out in each of the next four seasons.

The Braves had a winning record in each of those seasons. But none of those years could top 1957. Directed by new manager Fred Haney, the Braves won 95 games that season. They also won the NL pennant and advanced to the World Series. Hank Aaron was named the NL's MVP. Warren Spahn was named the Cy Young Award winner as baseball's best pitcher. The Braves had other stars, too. Eddie Mathews and Wes Covington posted great seasons on offense, and Lew Burdette and Bob Buhl backed up Spahn by winning a combined 35 games on the mound.

During the World Series, the Braves played the defending champion New York Yankees—a team that had won the championship 17 times since 1923. This was the Braves' year, though. They defeated the Yankees four games to three to

Braves pitcher Lew Burdette fires the final pitch of the 1957 World Series at Yankee Stadium. The Braves beat the Yankees to win the title.

win their first championship since 1914. Burdette pitched a shutout in Game 7 at Yankee Stadium as the Braves beat the Yankees 5–0. Aaron hit .393 with three homers and seven runs batted in (RBIs) during the Series. Burdette won all three games he pitched, shutting out the Yankees in the final 24 innings he pitched. "He's the best pitcher we've faced," Yankees manager Casey Stengel said of Burdette. "Nobody I've seen since I took over this club has stopped us this way."

As good as the Braves were in 1957, there appeared to be more winning to come. "This was the year to beat the

Braves," Cardinals general manager Frank Lane said. "Next year, I'm afraid they'll be unstoppable."

The Braves lived up to the hype. In 1958, they were nearly unstoppable. The team won 92 games in the regular season. Like the year before, they faced the Yankees in the World Series. They took a three games to one lead in the Series. The Yankees took over from there, however. The Yankees won the final three games to take the championship. "Had we hit when it counted, it would have been a different story," Haney said.

The next season, the Braves nearly made it to another World Series. But this time, they lost to the Los Angeles Dodgers in a best-of-three playoff. Aaron, Mathews, Spahn, and Burdette had great seasons once again for the Braves. But for the first time in three years, they would not be going to the World Series.

All seemed to be well with the Braves in Milwaukee. But what started off as such a good marriage between the Braves and the city was about to end very poorly. The Braves set attendance records in their early years in Milwaukee, but they saw attendance fall in the

The Milwaukee Mauler

For most of Eddie Mathews's career, he played with one of the greatest players in major league history—Hank Aaron. Mathews had a great career of his own, however. He played for the Braves from 1952 to 1966. He is the only player to play for the team when it was based in Boston, Milwaukee, and Atlanta. Mathews finished his career with 512 home runs. He was an All-Star in nine of his seasons and was elected to the Hall of Fame in 1978. Mathews also has the distinction of being on the cover of the first-ever issue of Sports Illustrated, *on August 16, 1954.*

Braves outfielder Hank Aaron sprints deep alongside the vine-covered wall at Wrigley Field to catch a ball against the Chicago Cubs in 1958.

1960s. With the Braves losing money, they announced in 1964 plans to leave Milwaukee. They wanted to move to Atlanta, Georgia, for the 1965 season. However, they were forced to fulfill a contract to play in Milwaukee in 1965. "Even if we have to play in Milwaukee, our hearts will be in Atlanta,"

Milwaukee or Atlanta Braves?

In 1965, the Braves were still in Milwaukee, but everybody knew they were going to Atlanta in 1966. Atlanta was already preparing for the team's arrival. Several Braves games were broadcast on TV and radio in Atlanta. In fact, fans in Atlanta saw more Braves games on TV than fans in Milwaukee did in 1965.

Braves executive vice president Thomas A. Reynolds Jr. said.

In the end, the Braves got their way. But they still had to play one final, awkward season in Milwaukee. "It was a terrible thing for it all to end that way, because we had something special in Milwaukee," Spahn said.

Aaron also noted, "To this day, whenever I'm in Milwaukee, which is often, I'm reminded that the people there still haven't gotten over the Braves leaving. If it helps, they should know that the players haven't either."

Stellar Southpaw

Warren Spahn won more games (363) than any left-handed pitcher in major league history. He was a permanent part of the Braves pitching rotation from 1946 to 1964. He led the league in wins eight times. Spahn was inducted into the Baseball Hall of Fame in 1973 and is one of six Braves to have their numbers retired by the team. Spahn was also a war hero, which is why he did not pitch from 1943 to 1945. For his service in World War II, he was awarded a Bronze Star and a Purple Heart.

Long before he was managing the New York Yankees to four World Series titles, Joe Torre was a top young catcher for the Braves from 1960 to 1968.

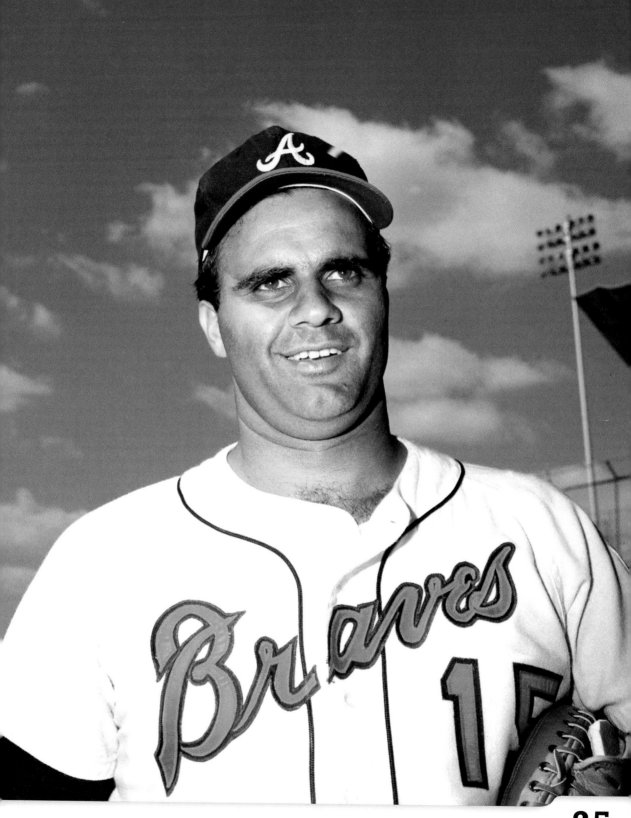

CHAPTER 4

FINDING A NEW HOME

The Braves received a warm welcome when they arrived in Atlanta. That was in part because MLB was new to that area of the country. "It didn't take long to realize also that we were playing for an entire section of the country," Hank Aaron said. More than 50,000 fans attended the Braves' first official game in Atlanta, on April 12, 1966.

During their first season in Atlanta, the Braves posted their 14th consecutive winning season. But they still had not been to the postseason since 1958. That drought would end in their fourth season in the southeast in 1969.

Bringing His Bat

On July 3, 1966, Braves pitcher Tony Cloninger had a day that most hitters only dream about. He became the first player in NL history to hit two grand slams in one game. On that day, he had three hits, nine RBIs, and pitched a complete game in a 17–3 Braves win against the Giants in San Francisco.

Braves pitcher Tony Cloninger poses with an armload of baseball bats the day after he hit two grand slams and pitched a complete game against the San Francisco Giants in 1966.

Phil Niekro, the only knuckleballer to win 300 games, collected 23 wins in the 1969 season. He was inducted into the Hall of Fame in 1997.

Before 1969, only the AL and NL champions qualified for the playoffs. In 1969, however, each league was split into two divisions. After that, the two division winners in each league qualified for the playoffs. That added an extra round in the postseason, giving more teams a chance to compete for the pennants.

The Braves benefited from the new rule right away. They had the second-best record in

Hanging Around

Pitcher Phil Niekro perfected the knuckleball in the minor leagues and turned it into a 24-year major league career. He played for the Braves in all but three of those seasons, and he retired at age 48. Niekro won 318 games during his career, including 121 after his fortieth birthday.

the NL, but won the West division championship. Led by Aaron, Orlando Cepeda, and Rico Carty, the Braves won 93 games. Future Hall of Fame pitcher Phil Niekro won 23 games that season.

Once in the playoffs, the Braves ran into the "Amazin' Mets." The New York Mets had won 100 games that season. They had no trouble getting past the Braves, outscoring them 27–15 in a three-game sweep.

"The Mets jumped all over us in the '69 playoffs, and when they were through, we knew we'd been up against more than we could handle," Aaron said. "We didn't necessarily believe that they were the better team, but we knew that nothing was going to stop them."

That was the last time the great Hank Aaron would play in the playoffs. It would also be 13 years before the Braves would get back. From 1970 to 1981, the Braves had just three winning seasons. During the early part of the 1970s, however, they did have Aaron to rally around. His quest for the career home-run record, which he set April 8, 1974, was one of baseball's main attractions.

The 1970s produced a few other good moments for the

Turner Takes Over

Ted Turner was a well-known yachtsman and television tycoon. But in 1976, he became known for buying the Braves for $11 million. Turner did not know much about baseball until his Atlanta television station began broadcasting Braves games in 1973. A few years later, fans around the country were able to watch Braves games on Turner's WTBS channel. In his early days of owning the team, Turner endeared himself to fans by taking part in wacky stunts, such as a mattress-stuffing contest and a motorized bathtub race.

Braves. In 1970, outfielder Carty won the NL batting title and posted a 31-game hitting streak. He missed the entire 1971 season with a leg injury, however, and was never the same player again. Also in 1970, Aaron collected the 3,000th hit of his career.

Niekro threw a no-hitter on August 5, 1973, shutting out the San Diego Padres 9–0. Niekro was a Brave from 1964 to 1983. Also in the 1970s, the Braves had two players win the Rookie of the Year Award. They were Earl Williams in 1971 and Bob Horner in 1978.

Despite struggling for more than a decade, the Braves came into 1982 with high hopes. "We can win the division. It isn't beyond the realm of possibility," first baseman Chris Chambliss said. Outfielder Dale Murphy added, "It's about time for us to do something. We had a chance [in 1981], but then something happened. We played bad."

The Braves did not play bad in 1982. In fact, they won their first 13 games of the season—a major league record. They beat the Los Angeles Dodgers to win the NL West Division cham-pionship and earned a playoff spot for the first time since 1969. Once in the playoffs, they

Murphy Repeats

One of the most popular and most respected players in Braves history was Dale Murphy. He played for the team from 1976 to 1990. Murphy was named the NL's MVP in 1982 and in 1983. He became the only Brave to win the award twice and one of just six NL players to win it two years in a row. A catcher and first baseman early in his career, he found a home as an outfielder in 1980 and later won five Gold Gloves for his great defense. Joe Torre, who managed the Braves from 1982 to 1984, said, "All he does is play baseball better than anyone else." Murphy's No. 3 jersey is one of six retired by the Braves.

Catcher Bruce Benedict and pitcher Rick Camp embrace after the Braves beat the Houston Astros to start the 1982 season with 11 straight wins.

were no match for the NL East champion St. Louis Cardinals, however. The Braves lost all three games of the NL Championship Series (NLCS). Still, it was a successful season. "We came too far to be disappointed," veteran Jerry Royster said.

Reaching the playoffs in 1982 failed to serve as a springboard to more success. The Braves finished second in the NL West in 1983. After that, they posted seven straight losing seasons from 1984 to 1990. In 1988, 1989, and 1990, the Braves were the worst team in the NL. That was about to change.

CHAPTER 5

YEARS OF DOMINANCE

Despite coming into 1991 with three consecutive last-place finishes, there was a sense that the Braves would improve. The team already had young talent. That off-season it had signed some veterans to complement them. Few expected the Braves to contend for the NL West championship, but they had done enough to make their opponents worry.

"Atlanta can't be overlooked," San Francisco Giants general manager Al Rosen said before the 1991 season. "I've always thought Bobby Cox was an excellent manager, and he's got impact players in [Ron] Gant and [David] Justice."

Rosen did have reason to worry. Justice was the NL Rookie of the Year in 1990 and backed it up with another great season in 1991. Gant was one of the best all-around outfielders in the game. Outfielder Otis Nixon had a great year, too.

The Braves celebrate their NLCS win over the Pittsburgh Pirates in 1991 to advance to the World Series against the Minnesota Twins.

Terry Pendleton, one of the veterans signed in the off-season, had such a great year that he was named the 1991 NL MVP. Tom Glavine led the pitching staff. He won 20 games and was voted the NL's Cy Young Award winner. Charlie Leibrandt, John Smoltz, and Steve Avery backed up Glavine by winning a combined 47 games.

That group made the leap from worst in the NL in 1990 to first in the West Division in 1991. "That's why this is the world's greatest game," second baseman Jeff Blauser said. "We were down and out, but we battled back. And now, we're here."

Prior to 1991, no team in the twentieth century had ever gone from last place one year to first place the next. In 1991, two teams did it—the Braves and the Minnesota Twins of the AL West. The two wound up meeting in the World Series, and some have called that Series the greatest ever. Five of the seven games were decided by a single run. Three of the games, including the final two, went into extra innings.

The Twins won the championship by scoring in the 10th inning of Game 7 for a 1–0 victory. Despite their best effort, the Braves had to settle for

Braves second baseman Mark Lemke scores the game-winning run in the ninth inning of the fourth game of the 1991 World Series.

second place. "Tell [the Braves fans] we gave it everything we had," said second baseman Mark Lemke, whose .417 batting average was the best of any player in the Series. "Tell them we gave our hearts this season."

The 1991 season was just the start of a remarkable run of success for the Braves. The Braves won 14 consecutive division championships from 1991 to 2005. That streak is unmatched in baseball history. The Braves also advanced to the World Series five times during those years.

Throughout that streak, the Braves had several great

players leave. Yet they always found ways to replace them. Pendleton, Gant, Justice, and first baseman Sid Bream were all gone by 1997. In their places, the Braves found star players such as Fred McGriff, Ryan Klesko, Marquis Grissom, Brian Jordan, Gary Sheffield, Chipper Jones, Javy Lopez, Andruw Jones, and Rafael Furcal.

Two things did not change. First was manager Bobby Cox. He took over as Braves' manager during the 1990 season and led the team through 2010. Second, the Braves always had great pitching.

Prior to 1991, the Braves had one Cy Young Award winner. That was Warren Spahn in 1957. During an eight-year span from 1991 to 1998, Braves pitchers won six Cy Young Awards. Two of those were by Tom Glavine, in 1991 and 1998; one was by John Smoltz in 1996; and Greg Maddux won three in a row from 1993 to 1995. The Braves had other great pitchers during their run of success. However, Glavine, Maddux, and Smoltz were the stars of the staff.

Although the Braves won 14 straight division titles from 1991 to 2005, they had trouble winning the World Series.

Steal of a Deal

The Braves did not start their string of dominance until 1991, but they began preparing for it years before that. On August 12, 1987, the Braves made one of the most significant trades in team history when they sent Doyle Alexander, a journeyman 36-year-old pitcher, to the Detroit Tigers for minor league pitcher John Smoltz. Alexander played two more seasons before retiring. Smoltz played for the Braves from 1988 to 2008 and compiled 210 wins and 154 saves while also winning the 1996 NL Cy Young Award.

Between them, *from left*, Tom Glavine, John Smoltz, and Greg Maddux won six Cy Young Awards between 1991 and 1998 for the Braves.

The Braves won just one championship during that time. It came in 1995. That was the first season MLB went to the wild-card system for the playoffs. Since the AL and NL each had three divisions, the division champions as well as the next best team—the wild card—made the playoffs.

In 1995, the Braves had to get through the Colorado Rockies and Cincinnati Reds in the NL playoffs. They then defeated the AL-champion Cleveland Indians in the World Series, four games to two. Glavine went 2–0 during the Series, including a win in the final game. He was named the Series MVP.

Eventually, the Braves' streak came to an end. Glavine left for the New York Mets in 2003. Maddux left for the Chicago Cubs in 2004. Others retired or were traded. The rest of the division finally began catching up to Atlanta, too. The Braves' reign came to an end in 2006, when they finished third in the NL East. It was the team's first losing record in 16 years. The Braves had winning records in 2007 and 2009, but missed out on the playoffs.

Before the 2010 season, Cox announced that he was coming back to coach the Braves for one more year. It became a resurgent year in Atlanta. Young players such as rookie outfielder Jason Heyward, catcher Brian McCann, and infielder Martin Prado combined with veterans

Sid's Slide Home

During Game 7 of the 1992 NLCS, the Braves needed a miracle to pull off a win. They trailed the Pittsburgh Pirates 2–0 going into the bottom of the ninth inning. After pulling within 2–1, the Braves were down to their last out. But they also had the bases loaded. To the plate stepped backup first baseman Francisco Cabrera, who had played in only 12 games that season. Cabrera delivered the Braves' miracle, hitting a single to left field. David Justice scored the tying run easily, and Sid Bream, Atlanta's slow, 32-year-old first baseman, lumbered around third base. Pittsburgh outfielder Barry Bonds threw home and Bream slid into the plate—barely beating the tag and giving the Braves a 3–2 win that sent them to the 1992 World Series.

such as pitchers Tim Hudson and Billy Wagner to win the wild card. However, the Braves could not get past the San Francisco Giants in the NL Division Series (NLDS).

The Atlanta Braves celebrate after beating the Cleveland Indians 1–0 on October 28, 1995, to become World Series champions.

TEAM LEADERS

Three pitchers and two field players defined the Braves during the 1990s and early 2000s. Pitchers Tom Glavine, Greg Maddux, and John Smoltz combined to win the NL Cy Young Award six times in eight years. That trio was together in Atlanta from 1993 to 2002. During those 10 seasons, they won 453 games and combined for 15 All-Star appearances. Smoltz later went to the bullpen and added 65 saves.

Outfielder Andruw Jones and third baseman/outfielder Chipper Jones were teammates on the Braves from 1996 to 2007. Andruw Jones burst onto the scene during the 1996 World Series. As a 19-year-old, he belted two home runs in the Series. In a Braves uniform from 1996 to 2007, he hit 368 home runs and won 10 consecutive Gold Gloves for his defense in center field. Chipper Jones became a starter for the Braves in 1995. He reached six All-Star Games and won the NL MVP award in 1999.

The Giants won the series three games to one.

A strong core group of players remained, but the team would have to continue on without their iconic manager who had been there since 1990. Cox finished with 2,504 wins during 29 years as a manager, good for fourth all-time.

The Braves have had their ups and downs. Through it all they have always managed to provide their fans with exhilarating moments and All-Star players. Some teams have more championships, and others have had more Hall of Famers, but few teams have enjoyed the rich history of the Braves.

Braves manager Bobby Cox tips his hat to the hometown fans after his final game, a loss to the San Francisco Giants in the 2010 NLDS.

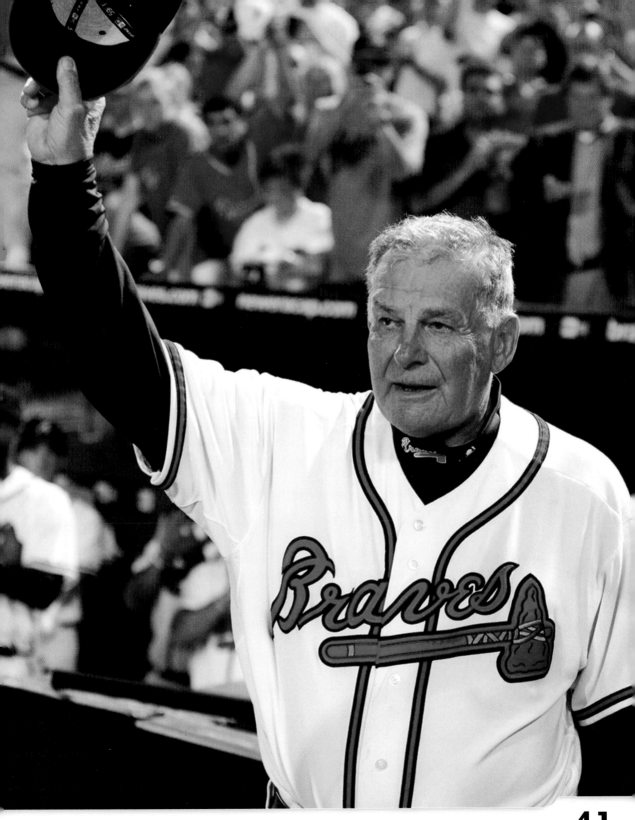

TIMELINE

1876	The Boston Red Caps join the newly formed NL. They play the first game in NL history, on April 22, 1876, defeating the Philadelphia Athletics.
1898	The Boston Beaneaters win their eighth NL championship since 1877. It is their final championship of the nineteenth century.
1912	The team adopts the name Braves.
1914	The Braves surge from last place in July to win the NL pennant. They sweep the favored Athletics to win the World Series for the first time.
1948	Behind pitchers Warren Spahn and Johnny Sain, the Braves reach the World Series but lose to the Cleveland Indians.
1953	Playing their first season in Milwaukee, the Braves draw an NL-record 1,826,397 fans to Milwaukee County Stadium.
1957	In one of the best seasons in team history, the Braves win the NL pennant and defeat the New York Yankees in the World Series. Hank Aaron is named NL MVP and Warren Spahn wins the Cy Young Award.
1965	Losing fans in Milwaukee, the Braves attempt to move to Atlanta, but a court order forces them to play one last season in Milwaukee.
1966	After 13 seasons in Milwaukee, the Braves make their debut in Atlanta.

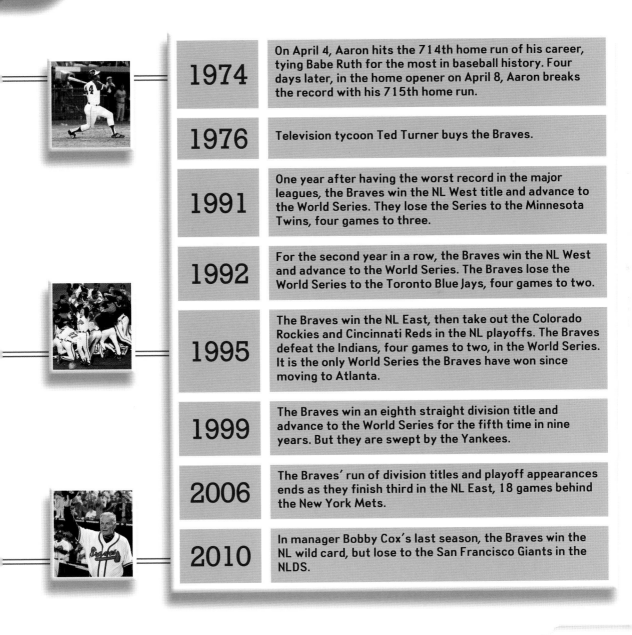

1974 On April 4, Aaron hits the 714th home run of his career, tying Babe Ruth for the most in baseball history. Four days later, in the home opener on April 8, Aaron breaks the record with his 715th home run.

1976 Television tycoon Ted Turner buys the Braves.

1991 One year after having the worst record in the major leagues, the Braves win the NL West title and advance to the World Series. They lose the Series to the Minnesota Twins, four games to three.

1992 For the second year in a row, the Braves win the NL West and advance to the World Series. The Braves lose the World Series to the Toronto Blue Jays, four games to two.

1995 The Braves win the NL East, then take out the Colorado Rockies and Cincinnati Reds in the NL playoffs. The Braves defeat the Indians, four games to two, in the World Series. It is the only World Series the Braves have won since moving to Atlanta.

1999 The Braves win an eighth straight division title and advance to the World Series for the fifth time in nine years. But they are swept by the Yankees.

2006 The Braves' run of division titles and playoff appearances ends as they finish third in the NL East, 18 games behind the New York Mets.

2010 In manager Bobby Cox's last season, the Braves win the NL wild card, but lose to the San Francisco Giants in the NLDS.

QUICK STATS

FRANCHISE HISTORY
Boston Red Caps (1876–82)
Boston Beaneaters (1883–1906)
Boston Doves (1907–10)
Boston Rustlers (1911)
Boston Braves (1912–35)
Boston Bees (1936–40)
Boston Braves (1941–52)
Milwaukee Braves (1953–65)
Atlanta Braves (1966–)

WORLD SERIES
(wins in bold)
1914, 1948, **1957,** 1958, 1991, 1992,
1995, 1996, 1999

NL CHAMPIONSHIP SERIES
(1969–)
1969, 1982, 1991, 1992, 1993, 1995,
1996, 1997, 1998, 1999, 2001

KEY PLAYERS
(position[s]; seasons with team)
Henry "Hank" Aaron (OF; 1954–74)
Hugh Duffy (OF; 1892–1900)
Tom Glavine (SP; 1987–2002, 2008)
Chipper Jones (3B/OF; 1993, 1995–)
Greg Maddux (SP; 1993–2003)
Rabbit Maranville (SS/2B; 1912–20,
    1929–35)
Eddie Mathews (3B/1B; 1952–66)
Kid Nichols (SP; 1890–1901)
Phil Niekro (SP; 1964–83, 1987)
John Smoltz (SP/RP; 1988–99,
    2001–08)
Warren Spahn (SP; 1942, 1946–64)

KEY MANAGERS
Bobby Cox (1978–81, 1990–2010):
    2,149–1,709; 64–65 (postseason)
Frank Selee (1890–1901):
    1,004–649

HOME FIELDS
South End Grounds (1876–1914)
Fenway Park (1915)
Braves Field (1915–52)
Milwaukee County Stadium
    (1953–65)
Atlanta-Fulton County Stadium
    (1966–96)
Turner Field (1997–)

*Statistics through 2010 season

QUOTES AND ANECDOTES

Cy Young may be the greatest pitcher to ever play baseball, Babe Ruth may be the greatest hitter to ever play, and Jim Thorpe may be the greatest all-around athlete the world has ever seen. They have something else in common, too: All three played their final few major league games with the Braves. Young finished his 22-year career by pitching 11 games for the Boston Rustlers in 1911, at the age of 44. Ruth finished his 22-year career by playing 28 games for the Boston Braves in 1935, at the age of 40. Thorpe, more well known as an Olympic gold medalist and a Hall of Fame football player, played the final 60 games of his baseball career for the Boston Braves in 1919, at age 32.

"Period. It's time."—Bobby Cox, after signing a one-year contract extension to manage the Braves for a 25th and final season in 2010. Cox managed the Braves to 2,149 regular season wins, five NL pennants, and the 1995 World Series.

For years, the Braves had one of the most devoted fans in the major leagues. That tradition began with the minor league teams that played in Atlanta before the Braves arrived. Pearl Sandow, a native of Canton, Georgia, attended every professional game in Atlanta except for one from 1934 to 1989. She attended every home Braves game from 1966 to 1989—a streak of 1,889 straight games—until an accident in 1990 left her with two broken shoulders. After that, she watched the Braves on television or listened to them on the radio. In 1989, she was enshrined in the fan section of the National Baseball Hall of Fame in Cooperstown, New York. Sandow passed away in 2006 at the age of 103.

GLOSSARY

consecutive

Things that follow one another in uninterrupted succession or order.

consistency

Holding together and keeping form.

exhibition

A game in which the teams play to develop skills and promote the sport rather than for a competitive advantage.

franchise

An entire sports organization, including the players, coaches, and staff.

free agent

A player whose contract has expired and who is able to sign with a team of his choice.

general manager

The executive who is in charge of the team's overall operation. He or she hires and fires managers and coaches, drafts players, and signs free agents.

legendary

Well known and admired over a long period.

pennant

A flag. In baseball, it symbolizes that a team has won its league championship.

postseason

The games in which the best teams play after the regular-season schedule has been completed.

retire

To officially end one's career.

rookie

A first-year player in the major leagues.

tycoon

A businessperson with great power or wealth.

wild card

Playoff berths given to the best remaining teams that did not win their respective divisions.

FOR MORE INFORMATION

Further Reading

Glavine, Tom, with Nick Cafardo. *None But the Braves: A Pitcher, A Team, A Champion.* New York: HarperCollins Publishers, 1996.

Stanton, Tom. *Hank Aaron and the Home Run That Changed America.* New York: W. Morrow, 2004.

Vecsey, George. *Baseball: A History of America's Favorite Game.* New York: Modern Library, 2008.

Web Links

To learn more about the Atlanta Braves, visit ABDO Publishing Company online at **www.abdopublishing.com**. Web sites about the Braves are featured on our Book Links page. These links are routinely monitored and updated to provide the most current information available.

Places to Visit

Atlanta Braves Museum and Hall of Fame
755 Hank Aaron Drive
Atlanta, GA 30315
404-614-2311
mlb.mlb.com/atl/ballpark/museum.jsp
This museum has more than 600 historical items from the team's history. It is open year-round.

National Baseball Hall of Fame and Museum
25 Main Street
Cooperstown, NY 13326
888-HALL-OF-FAME
www.baseballhall.org
This hall of fame and museum highlights the greatest players and moments in the history of baseball. Hank Aaron, Eddie Mathews, Phil Niekro, and Warren Spahn are among the former Braves enshrined here.

Turner Field
755 Hank Aaron Drive
Atlanta, GA 30315
404-614-2311
mlb.mlb.com/atl/ballpark/index.jsp
This has been the Braves' home field since 1997. Tours are available when the Braves are not playing.

INDEX

About the Author

Brian Howell is a freelance writer based in Denver, Colorado. He has been a sports journalist for more than 17 years, writing about high school and college athletics, as well as covering major professional sporting events such as the US Open golf tournament, the World Series, and the Stanley Cup playoffs. He has earned several writing awards during his career. A native of Colorado, he lives with his wife and four children in Colorado.